MAD LIBS®

TRAVEL FAR
AND MAD LIBS

by Anthony Casciano

MAD LIBS
An Imprint of Penguin Random House LLC, New York

Concept created by Roger Price & Leonard Stern

Cover illustration by Scott Brooks

Published by Mad Libs,
an imprint of Penguin Random House LLC, New York.
Printed in the USA.

Visit us online at www.penguinrandomhouse.com.

ISBN 9781524792237
7 9 10 8